MW01615382

ELLA SPEAKS FRENCH & CONQUERS WINTER

ELLA SPEAKS FRENCH & CONQUERS WINTER

A Bilingual Adventure

Book 2

Lucie Angers

Copyright © 2024 by Lucie Angers

All rights reserved. No part of this publication may be reproduced, distributed, or transmitted in any form or by any means, including photocopying, recording, or other methods, without the prior written permission of the author, except in the case of brief quotations embodied in published reviews.

ISBN PAPERBACK: 978-1-7382343-2-5

Published by ELLA parle français
Montreal, Quebec, Canada.
Illustrations by Edgar Bridwell

This is a work of fiction. While some businesses and places mentioned in the story may exist, they have been chosen for narrative purposes and to provide an authentic atmosphere. Names, characters, events, and incidents are either the products of the author's imagination or used in a fictitious manner.

The book also contains language learning elements, and while efforts have been made to ensure accuracy and appropriateness, the author does not assume responsibility for any errors or omissions.

Reading and language learning are subjective experiences, and individual results may vary. The author only intends for this book to serve as a helpful tool for learners and a source of enjoyment.

Contact information: info@ellaparlefrancais.com
www.ellaparlefrancais.com

DEDICATION

Why "Ella"? I've been asked.

Well, it's a nod to my late father, undoubtedly the person I admired most. During his lifetime, he founded a (very serious) IT company, and he cleverly and playfully incorporated his own initials into its name.

True to his youthful spirit, I'll leave you with the fun task of saying my own initials out loud, with a French pronunciation.

Let's all celebrate our alter egos.

With *amour*,

Lucie Angers

TABLE OF CONTENTS

19 - DIX-NEUF :
J'ARRIVE

This bed is so comfy and warm. I'd like to stay here all day. In fact, I think I may never leave this bed. Reality is too difficult. *Adulting* is not for me. I just want to stay here and feel sorry for myself. Why did I have to leave Seattle and come to an unknown city by myself, a French city to top it off?

It's not easy. I can't learn French anymore. I miss home. And I miss *him*… All. Of. This.

Before arriving in Montreal, or **Montréal** as I should say, I'd met this guy… this very nice guy. We had some mutual friends, and the story began like this: there was a house party; I was bored; this cute guy walked in; we started talking; I instantly felt comfortable with him, and we were like old friends; we confided in each other about stories from our past and shared tons of laughs together; we talked about dreams we had, projects we had planned, things we loved or hated. It was easy.

After that party, we got together and went on several dates. Thinking back, I'm not sure they were *actual* dates, but they felt like that to me. We would ride our bikes along the waterfront on the Elliott Bay Trail, stop for ice cream at the Pike Place Market and watch the sunset. We would wander around the city, window shop at all the vintage shops and galleries we could find, go to Starbucks, relax in parks or at the beach.

Maybe we were just friends, but my feelings for him grew, naturally. Being with him was unquestionably so comfortable, so easy... at the time. Did I mention that this was **avant**, before Montréal, when I was still in **Seattle,** where speaking English was the norm? Ugh.

French. **Français.** Because I barely speak français, everything is more difficult here **à** Montréal. Avant, it was easy. Now, simple interactions become complex. Asking for directions is exhausting enough, so you can imagine how making friends seems almost inconceivable. And today, after a grueling two-week period trying to learn that language, I've come to realize that I am *done*! I just want to stay under these warm blankets and avoid freezing in the Montréal winter, speaking français or dealing with a different culture. My goal is to simply not move, and to keep reminiscing about the good old times in Seattle when life was easier and when *he,* **il** was there. And yes, il was there for a while. A nice long summer. Until *she,* **elle** came back. The *ex,* of course. Precisely when I thought life was going so well for me, it turned around and slapped me in the face. I was broken-hearted and miserable, as miserable as I am today à Montréal.

— **Ella**? I hear through the door.
— Yes? I mean: **Oui?** I reluctantly say.
— **Ça va, Ella?** Says the muffled voice.

It's **Monique,** checking up on me, making sure I am well. I've been staying at her house since day one à Montréal and although Monique is the nicest person, I wish she would leave

me alone today. Avant, it would have been fine, but today is Saturday, there is no class, why would I get up?

— Ella...? **Viens**, says Monique in a soft, almost mischievous tone.

I know « viens » means « come », but I do not want to do as I'm told. That would mean leaving the comfort of my bed and my sad state of mind. I know it's pathetic, but sometimes, I just want to stay that way. I don't want any change; I want to stay put. I want to dwell in my sadness. Besides, there is nothing better than staying in bed and sleeping in when it's cold outside.

You know the French expression « **faire la grasse matinée** »? Well, literally, it means « to do the fat morning ». I know, it's the weirdest thing. But, in a funny way, it means to stay in bed, to sleep in. Like a fat, thick or heavy sleep. And that's what I intend to do.

— Ellaaa...

I can faintly hear Monique repeat my name behind the door. Ugh. Really? Monique won't stop, will she. Well, it is her home.

— Oui, I'm on my way, **j'arrive**, I say unenthusiastically.

With great difficulty and a heavy sigh, I grab my sweater which is on top of the bed and rapidly put it on before the chilly air hits me. Can you tell I've been here for a while now? Now, I'm prepared! A warm sweater is always nice and handy.

As I take the few steps that separate my bed from the door, I hear another « Ellaaaaa... »

— Oui, Monique, j'arrive!

I turn the doorknob, reluctantly push the door open and what do I see? Monique with the biggest grin, hiding behind a pair of traditional wood snowshoes; « **des raquettes** », she exclaims. These things are huge!

— Des raquettes? I repeat pointing at the snowshoes.

— Oui, Ella. **Tu** viens?

Oh, no, no, no! **Non**. I am not coming. Today, is the day I feel sorry for myself. Not the day I follow Monique and go snowshoeing.

— **Je** viens? I grumble. I am *not* happy. « Non, Monique, non... »

— Oui, oui, viens Ella!

Monique is in a great mood. As she grabs **les** raquettes in one hand, in **une main**, she takes **ma** main with her other main and gently pulls me toward the kitchen. « Viens, **j'ai une surprise!** »

— **Tu as** une surprise?

What surprise could she have for me?

— Oui, j'ai une surprise. Une **grosse** surprise.

What big surprise could she have for me? Une grosse suprise? Aren't les raquettes big enough already? But I admit, her cheerful disposition is seriously contagious. I am curious now. She heads to the kitchen, skipping, leaving me trailing behind.

— Tu viens Ella?

— Oui, j'arrive!

J'arrive in the kitchen, and what do I see?

✳✳✳✳✳

« Tu as une surprise? »

20 - VINGT :
SURPRISE

This is not possible. My bestie, <u>Chloé</u>! My dear friend **française**, from Seattle. What is she doing here, à Montréal?
— Surprise! Monique yells. She smiles; elle **sourit**.
— Chloé! I let out a cry. I am so thrilled. « What are you doing here »?
— Je viens **te voir,** she says in her beautiful European **accent** français.
— You're here to see me? But… ça va? I try saying **en** français. Ça va **bien**?

I am struggling with my feelings. I am so happy to see her, but is everything fine? I mean, one minute ago, I'm miserable in my bed and the next, my best friend from Seattle is in my homestay, where I live à Montréal. That is insane!
— Oui, oui, ça va Ella.
— Everything is fine? Um… **Tout va bien**?
— Oui, Ella, tout va bien. Elle sourit, and she adds: Je **suis** en **vacances.**
— Vacation? For how long?

I can feel Monique's stare as all the words coming out of my mouth are in English. I'm forgetting all **mon** français, I'm too excited!
— Une **semaine** à Montréal. Chloé says as she is showing seven fingers.

Seven… days? So… one week? Yeah, I get it. How do I say *awesome* or *great* again? Oui, I remember: « **Génial!** » I exclaim cheerfully. « Tu viens **pour *deux* semaines**? » I joke, thinking that a two-week long stay would be so fun.

— Non… **juste** une semaine, replies Chloé. « Une **longue** semaine **de** vacances à Montréal. »

Now that I am reassured that tout va bien, I can truly be happy and express my joy to have her by my side. I jump toward her and give her the best hug. My dearest Chloé is here, in my arms. I am juste so happy, but I still can't quite believe it. Ma Chloé **est** à Montréal pour une longue semaine. I'm so happy I could scream!

Together, we are like deux little girls, as if we were six years old again, jumping up and down and giggling. Monique sourit as elle watches us. Elle looks so happy and pleased with that surprise. Une grosse surprise **géniale**, really!

She says: Ella, ça va? Chloé, elle **vient** te voir… génial, non?

— Oui Monique, ça va bien. **Très** bien.

And it's true; everything is going very well. I am glowing. To think that juste a short moment avant, I was desperate and now, tout va bien, très bien. Life is beautiful.

« Ma Chloé est à Montréal pour une longue semaine. »

21 - VINGT ET UN :
ELLE ET MOI

— So, this is your room? Niiiice! Although a little messy... Don't you have a closet or a dresser to put your clothes in? Or is this some crafty carpet...

Chloé and I, elle **et moi,** always tease each other. We've been besties for as long as I can remember.
— But Chloé, truly, you promise, all is well? You are actually here à Montréal pour une semaine, juste for fun?
— Oui Ella, I promise. Je suis à Montréal pour te voir. Being here to see you is a good reason, don't you think?
— Oui, Chloé.
— Elle est grosse la surprise, non?
— Oui, elle est très grosse, I really am in disbelief. You planned everything with Monique?
— Oui, oui, elle est géniale Monique. That was so funny to see your face, what a reaction.
— I can imagine haha! Tell me, you, **toi,** what are you going to do while you're here?
— Me? Moi? I have to work on Monday, here à Montréal. But today et tomorrow, it's toi et moi baby!
— Génial! What do we do?
— Well, to start: de la **raquette!**
— Really? **Vraiment?** Tu viens à Montréal pour faire de la raquette?
— Oui, vraiment. Je viens à Montréal pour faire de la raquette, et pour te voir, sweet little face.

— Oui, vraiment, toi et moi, we are going to be snowshoeing, **on va** faire de la raquette?

— Oh, oui, Ella. I want to enjoy Montréal, the snow, sports, **l'hiver**... Yes, winter! Why are you being so difficult? Come on: Smile! **Souris!**

Je souris, a little. But my heart is not in it. Oui, je suis très happy to see my friend but, at the same time, I don't really want to be here anymore. I hate l'hiver and I thought I would like to learn français but I feel like I can't do this anymore. I think I may have to quit...

— Ella, tu viens?

— Vraiment? Vraiment?? Non!

— Oui, Ella, vraiment. Viens, on va faire de la raquette et... She steps closer to me, grabs my face with une main and pecks me right on the nose. « Now, you feel better? Viens, I promise, it will do you good. »

How did she know I wasn't feeling great? I guess real friends don't need to talk.

✳✳✳✳✳

« *Oui, Ella, vraiment. Viens, on va faire de la raquette.* »

22 - VINGT-DEUX :
LA RAQUETTE

We could have taken the bus, but Monique insisted on driving. She doesn't own a car, but like almost everyone here, she's a member of **Communauto,** a Canadian carsharing company, here, à Montréal; she simply picks up a car when she needs it. Smart!

— Ella, tu vas faire de la raquette. C'est génial. **Marc**, il...
Well, mon français isn't good enough to be able to understand everything Monique says, but I am pretty sure she is saying how her son Marc used to go faire de la raquette when he was young. Maybe that's what she's saying. As if I cared...

Honestly, I chose to sit in the back seat, so Chloé et Monique could speak français et get to know each other. L'accent français de Chloé is quite different from Monique's. So interesting!

Chloé listens with interest to Monique telling her story, then turns over to me and says: « Marc, **hum**? »

But I wonder why are we talking about him? He is not even here. He is never here in fact. He used to be around, until he started hanging out with this tall model-type gorgeous looking girl who calls him « **chéri** ». But that's not my problem...
— Monique, Chloé asks her: Marc, il **fait** de la raquette?
— Oui, il fait de la raquette **chaque** semaine.

Every week? Vraiment? Je suis surprise.

— Hum… il vient **aujourd'hui**?
Today? Aujourd'hui? Chloé is talking to Monique. What are they doing? Non… Is Chloé trying to get him to join us? No way! I see Monique getting her phone. She hands it to my friend and tells her what to type… Oh, dear… They are texting Marc. Why? Non! We were doing fine, juste us girls.

— Bonjour Marc! Chloé says.
What? She did actually phone him. « Oui, bonjour. Je suis Chloé, je viens de Seattle et je suis **avec** Ella et Monique. On va faire de la raquette aujourd'hui. Tu viens avec **nous**? Oui… on va à **Cap-Saint-Jacques**. »

Good grief! Did she lose her mind? I am pretty sure she juste invited Marc to go snowshoeing with us aujourd'hui. Avec nous?
— What did you do? I ask her.
— **J'ai invité** Marc à faire de la raquette avec nous. **C'est** génial, non? Il vient. **Dans** 20 **minutes**.
— Il vient… **ici**? Here? I squeak. In 20 minutes?
— Oui, il fait de la raquette chaque semaine. C'est vraiment bien.

Ok, don't laugh, but my first reaction was to look in the rear-view mirror to see if my hair looked acceptable. I quickly shift my gaze and instead stare out the window.
Chloé sourit. She saw me checking my hair. Uh-oh! Elle knows me très bien.

I'm looking out the window… C'est l'hiver. As we drive away from the city, from my now familiar neighbourhood, I notice the streets are becoming wider and the houses are more and more distant from each other.

Less traffic, less pollution means everything is whiter, covered with some magical snow, de la **neige magique**. Even chaque road sign is half hidden with a layer of white snow, de la neige **blanche**. L'hiver, everything becomes quieter, as la neige muffles each and every sound. La neige blanche leaves its mark on everything it touches, making the landscape slightly mystical.

Low-rise factory buildings are now replacing homes. Cars are moving fast, even if there is still quite a bit of neige on the highway. In chaque lane, you can see deux parallel black lines, where la neige melted due to the passing tires. The rest is monochrome: de la neige blanche. Even the sound is undoubtedly distinct; the tires hitting the melting snow on the pavement with a swishing sound. It has a calming effect on me.

I see airport road signs. To think that I was ici avant, deux semaines ago. Juste deux semaines, yet it feels like years ago. It almost seems like another dimension, as if my own life continued the old way but I decided to leave and make a turn, à Montréal. Vraiment, I guess it could be worse. I sigh.

I see Monique, et elle sourit in the rear-view mirror. She glances at me. Je souris too.
— Merci Monique!

She looks overjoyed. Tout va bien. For now. I'm a lucky person after all.

I see a sign: Cap-Saint-Jacques. **On est arrivées!** That was quick, not even une hour, une **heure**. Monique is now parking the car. Is it time to eat yet? I'm already hungry. I am staring at the cooler we brought which is filled with yummy snacks, des **collations**.

« On fait de la raquette, then, **ensuite: les collations!** » says Chloé winking as she reads my mind.
But I want to eat now!
Ok, ok. I'll try to act like a grownup. I open the door. Brr. Je suis surprise; I forgot about the cold. We were nice and toasty in the car. I zip up.

It's so beautiful ici. I must take a photo, je **prends** une **photo**. The trees avec la neige blanche, it's so beautiful et magique.

— Ella, j'ai invité Marc. Ça va? Chloé asks me privately.
— Oui, oui, ça va, I reply evasively.
— Vraiment, ça te va? Is that all right with you?
— Oui, oui, ça *me* va...

But am I fooling myself? Every time I see Marc, I stumble with my steps, my words, my thoughts, everything! It must be those blue eyes... and that gorgeous smile.

« Are we taking our snowshoes with us, hum... on **prend nos raquettes?** » I go to ask Monique to change the subject.

— Oui, on **les** prend. She answers.

— Et les collations, on les prend? I add.

— Non. Monique sourit : On **revient** ici dans une heure.

In one hour, « on revient »… I start thinking…

— « Vient » is « come », et « revient » is « come back », says Chloé as she sees my puzzled look.

— Ah, génial! For good measure and some practice, I repeat what I understood et say the longue sentence: « On va faire de la raquette, et ensuite on revient et on prend nos collations. »

— Toi, Ella… Toi, **tu es** géniale, says a man's voice.

I turn around et… who is ici?

Yep. C'est Marc.

Marc est ici!

« On revient ici dans une heure. »

23 - VINGT-TROIS :
LA RANDONNÉE

Five kilometres, **cinq kilomètres**. Pour moi, c'est vraiment a big hike, une longue **randonnée.** Yes, I am proud to say that I did five kilometres of snowshoeing: **j'ai fait** cinq kilomètres de raquette et it was a roller-coaster of emotions.

D'abord, first, we all left together: Chloé, Monique, Marc, la « **chérie** » girl (Oui, she was with him… for a change!) et moi. I had brought des collations et I ate them, because, well, I couldn't wait, I was too hungry.

Also, I refused to take off some layers even though they all told me I was wearing too many clothes et that I would be hot. That's fine. I prefer being hot than cold.

Right now, **j'ai froid.** I am cold. I also took my phone to take des **photos**, my water bottle, a pair of mittens in case the ones I was wearing got wet, an extra sweater in case I got cold, my sunglasses, my Swiss army knife, et my coffee mug, obviously. It all fit in my backpack, so I was good to go.

— **Un *couteau suisse*?** Marc had questioned me when we were about to start la randonnée.
— Oui, un couteau suisse.
Of course, I am bringing it. I may need to use it, who knows? Why did he look surprised?

— Chéri, ça va, ça va! The super-tall super-gorgeous model-type girl had commanded Marc as she lightly tapped the tips of her fingers together and announced matter-of-factly: « Ella, c'est une **touriste**. **Normal**. » She then put her arm under his, while firmly pulling him away from me, leaving him speechless et clearly embarrassed.

Vraiment? I am a tourist, and it's normal? What does that even mean? I feel judged. D'abord, la « chérie » girl is not even from **Québec**. Her accent est français, juste like Chloé. I may not understand much en français, but I can recognize un accent français et un accent from Québec. Pour moi, this comment is plain weird. Who does she think elle est? C'est *normal*… Ugh!

I decided to let it go and instead, focus on la randonnée et my bestie Chloé et sweet Monique who kindly brought me ici à Cap-Saint-Jacques.
— Let's go! **On y va**! Said Chloé to break the silence.
— Oui, on y va! Responded Monique enthusiastically.

D'abord, I had to take une photo. It's so beautiful en hiver. And too bad if that makes me une touriste. C'est normal… hum.

Ensuite, we left and took the path, **le sentier** that Marc recommended. The tall gorgeous super-snobby model looking girl française led the way, followed closely by Marc, Chloé, then Monique et moi trailing behind. Walking avec des raquettes à neige was not an easy task. Monique had lent Chloé et moi traditional webbed snowshoes - made by North American Indigenous people - which were quite massive to be honest.

I felt like I was walking with the grace and lightness of Godzilla.

Marc et the super-tall super-pretty somewhat-abnormal girl were wearing des raquettes à neige which looked much lighter and ergonomic; they took off and left us way behind. Which was fine. I was not experienced, blaming les **grosses** raquettes which made each step feel heavier than the previous one.

Monique was quite the expert. She had the same grosses raquettes traditional, but she was moving along at a good speed and had to constantly stop when she caught up with us.

— **Tu as froid?** Monique asked me while mimicking someone who is freezing, hugging herself and rubbing her own upper arms and saying: « **Brrr**, **il fait froid.** »

— Non, ça va, merci Monique. Oui, il fait froid, it is cold, but **je n'ai pas froid,** I am not cold, not the least. Faire de la raquette was quite the sport and I was warming up quite dramatically. « Une **minute**, Monique, je prends une photo. C'est **magnifique** ici. » I added. I'm thinking that's the correct word for magnificient? Monique sourit. I'll take that as a oui.

Ensuite, we had to make several stops to adjust nos raquettes, to read the signs to make sure we were on the right sentier, to eat des collations (the best!), and to remove some clothes (oui, I was hot). And also, to find a tissue (Merci Monique). I will never leave home without a few: the cold, le froid pretty much equals having a runny nose. Now I know. C'est normal en hiver when il fait froid. Lol.

Well, I must admit, la randonnée was amazing. I can now say that j'ai fait de la raquette, for the first time. J'ai fait cinq kilomètres. Vraiment, it should have been une heure, but, what's the rush? It took us nearly deux **heures**. By *us*, I mean nous: Chloé, Monique et moi. La chérie et le chéri? Who cares.

What is more important is this: la **température** was minus ten degrees Celsius. Oui, you read that right: **moins dix degrés Celsius.** That's 14 degrés Fahrenheit. Et, it didn't feel froid, juste invigorating.

We had to d'abord walk dans un sentier, which was surrounded by trees, bare dark brown trees stretching their branches toward the blue sky and above our heads, making le sentier feel like a tunnel with a nice thick carpet de neige blanche.

Then, ensuite, after a few stops, on est arrivées dans a small clearing. Ici, la neige blanche was like a screen onto which the shadows of the trees were projected. As the late afternoon sun was now low, the shadows were vraiment long and skinny, contrasting sharply with la neige. It was magique.

« *La neige blanche.* »

24 - VINGT-QUATRE :
LE CHOCOLAT

We are now back at the car. Chloé et Monique are *attacking* their collations as if they hadn't eaten in weeks.
— Tu ne **manges** pas, Ella? Asked Chloé. Are you not eating?
— Non, **euh**, how do you say: I've eaten?
— **J'ai mangé**. Says Chloé.
— So, oui, j'ai mangé **mes** collations.
— Tu as *tout* mangé? Everything?
— Oui, j'ai tout mangé.

Chloé sourit. She knows I like my food. And if I am stressed out, I definitely need to eat. Talking about stress, Marc is walking toward moi.
— Tu ne manges pas, Ella?
— Non, ça va, j'ai mangé.
— Tu veux **du chocolat**?

Did he say chocolate? I can never say no to du chocolat.
— **Merci**, thanks. I say timidly, putting out ma main.
He gives me a big piece et turns to la chérie.
— Et toi?
— Non, merci. She says with a pouting face.
Seriously, who doesn't like le chocolat? Ça, c'est normal?
Marc hands out du chocolat to everyone (well, except we-know-who), il sourit et asks me:
— Tu as froid Ella?
— Non…

I'm trying to think what to say. I *know* this. I don't want to say « je n'ai pas froid », because I *am* hot. It's not the same as not being cold...

So, what is the opposite of *froid*? Come on brain, do your stuff. I knew this word. What is it again? Bingo! « **Chaud** » is the word I need. And I am a girl, so the feminine version should be: **chaude**. And « I am » is « je suis ». Ella, you rock, if I can say so myself. So, super proudly I say to everyone: « Je suis chaude. »

Well, I admit, my amazing answer didn't get the success I expected. Everyone is laughing. And I mean, everyone. Laughing hard. Especially Marc. He's laughing uncontrollably. What did I do wrong? What did I say?

Chloé sourit, touches my shoulder with her forefinger and does a « tttsss » sound, as if she just burned her finger. « You're hot all right! » She exclaims laughing, clearly joking, as if I was hot to the touch. I turn around. I don't understand the joke.

Monique comes close to me and whispers: « *J'ai chaud.* »

What? I can feel my face turning red. I'm so lost right now. Everybody is having a good laugh, except me. This is juste a small mistake. Why is everybody laughing?

This hurts a little. A lot. I swallow my pride, try to smile, but I can't. Now everyone is talking all at once and I have no clue what they are saying. Oh man. I want out. I can feel my eyes watering and it's not because of the cold.

— Ella? Prends un chocolat, says Marc. Il sourit, softly, not arrogantly. His deep blue eyes are looking at me, kindly. I try to look elsewhere, but il insists. « Prends le chocolat. »

I look for Chloé but she's too busy giggling with Monique. I'm really trying to stop myself from sobbing now. « Non merci, Marc. Ça va. » He seems disappointed that he didn't know how to help. But he did help. After all, I'm not crying...

— Ella? This time it's Chloé. Don't make such a face. We're just teasing you, sweety. Your français is doing great, but you can't know everything right away. It's a process Ella...
— Oui, I know. But it's so frustrating. It's hard! Why were you all laughing?
— It's nothing. It's just that in English, you say « I'm hot ». But if you translate literally to « Je suis chaude », it means that you're... up for it, you're enthusiastic, excited about something. And, depending on the context, the « it » could be, you know... « it », like... you know... she added giggling.
— Hum... « it »? Oh dear... Everyone has a twisted mind.
— Yeah, it's funny, that's all.
— Funny?
— Oui, Ella, viens ici.

Chloé proceeds to give me a big hug.

— There, there Ella.
— Oh... That feels good. Merci.
— Better? Let's go to the car. On y va?
— Oui, on y va.

« *Ella? Prends un chocolat.* »

— And remember, en français, you « *have* heat » and you say: « J'ai chaud. »

— J'ai chaud. I repeat. Merci bien for the explanation.

— By the way, Monique was also telling me that « Je suis chaud » (if you're a guy) or « Je suis chaude » (if you're a girl) also means, ici in Québec, that you are drunk!

— Drunk? What? Okay, that's funny. I am not drunk!

— Hahaha, no, you're not.

But then Chloé winks at me and says: « Unless... you're drunk in love? »

Ugh. Why, oh why does this girl know everything that is going on in my head? Of course not, I'm not in love. But there is a feeling. And elle knows. Besties simply know it all.

25 - VINGT-CINQ :
AUJOURD'HUI

We are back in the Communauto car. I am sitting in the back seat again, curled up but with my wet boots off the seat so as not to dirty it. Aujourd'hui was a tough day.

D'abord, « je n'ai pas froid », is a nice sentence. Why didn't I juste say that? Or, I could have said : il ne fait pas froid. I knew that one Non... I had to be creative, original, I had to look smart. Sure. And now « Je suis chaude »... didn't mean what I wanted to say. Ugh! I ran into a double entendre inadvertently and now everyone thinks I have the hots for the only guy present, or that I don't speak français at all. I don't know which is worse.

Ensuite, j'ai vraiment froid. I really am cold now. I was hot during la randonnée et now j'ai froid in the car? What is this new world I live in? Is everything backward? It's different, **différent**. Everything is different, tout est différent, evidently.

But, I must admit, the scenery **était** magnifique et avec la neige blanche, it was amazing, **c'était** génial. Oui, c'est l'hiver, la température était de moins dix degrés, yet **ce n'était pas** unpleasant. Vraiment, really, it wasn't that cold.
L'hiver est magique.

The craziest thing for me, I must say, was the sound. La neige was muffling all the sounds, and we found ourselves staying quiet, listening to our own breathing and the odd snap of a small branch breaking beneath nos raquettes.

I must have dozed off. As I feel une main on my shoulder, I hear Chloé softly say: « On est arrivées. »
— What time is it? I say half asleep.
— Il est cinq heures, says Chloé as she stretched the cinq fingers of sa main.

Wow. Time flies when you're sleeping.
— Cinq heures?
— Oui. Tu viens Ella?
— On y va. J'ai faim. I really am hungry.
— Tu as faim? You're always hungry Ella.

Je souris. My best friend est avec moi à Montréal, et j'ai fait de la raquette for the first time ever... I'm thankful for aujourd'hui, even if things got off to a shaky start. Life is magnifique.

« On est arrivées. Tu as faim? »

26 - VINGT-SIX :
LA PIZZA

Tonight, j'ai mangé. A lot. J'ai **beaucoup** mangé. I was starving after our day à faire de la raquette.

Monique had ordered some pizza, de la **pizza**. C'était génial. Of course, I covered mine with black pepper. The pizza was delicious. La pizza était **délicieuse**. J'ai mangé cinq...
— Chloé, what is « how do we say » en français. I whisper.
— « **Comment on dit** »
— Merci. Comment on dit « slices » en français?
— **Pointes**.
— Pointes?
— Oui, whispers Chloé. The pizza slices are pointy...
Hum... C'est différent! Le français is original... But I'm too full to argue, so I simply announce: « J'ai mangé cinq pointes! »

Monique sourit, pretending she didn't hear our *Frenglish*. After all, I am learning new words en français et now, finally, je souris. I can't scowl all day, can I?

Yep, I don't know if it was because of la pizza or simply the great company, but my good mood is back tonight.

In Québec, from what I've seen so far, it's customary to gather around the table, talk and enjoy the meal for a good while. Dinnertime seems to be the most important moment of the day.

« La pizza était **délicieuse**. »

So tonight, I was eating, talking, even making jokes and saying I was « hot » for la pizza délicieuse and making Monique et Chloé laugh. Yes, it was just us girls. Marc had to go with la « chérie » girl.

And now, Chloé et moi are back in my room, getting ready to sleep in the same bed juste like on a sleepover when we were kids. I quickly move to the window side, as I've gotten into the habit of looking out the window when I wake up.

— **Désolée** Ella, I'm sorry, I'm taking too much space in your bed, I'm a bit bigger now... Are you comfortable?
— Of course, Chloé, I'm so happy you're ici, c'est génial.
— Vraiment?
— Oui, vraiment.
— Et... you're okay, with the « j'ai chaud » jokes? I really didn't want to hurt your feelings. I'm sorry. Je suis désolée. I should have been more sensitive. You're all alone here, it must be hard.
— Ça va... I say, suddenly more emotional that I care to admit.
— Ella, tell me... Tu **aimes** bien Marc?

What? Do I love Marc?? J'**aime** Marc? Has Chloé gone insane?

— I don't love Marc, clearly, and I just met him, I say, as I bolt upright in bed.

Chloé promptly grabs my arms, gently. Elle sourit.
— I know, I know, je **sais**, je sais. Let me explain a little français to you.

« Tu aimes Marc » means you *love* him.
« Tu aimes *bien* Marc » means you *like* him.

— What? But « bien » means « well », non? That doesn't make any sense!
— Je sais. But here's how it works en français. C'est différent. Let's say that when love is pure or real, it's on its own. If you say « j'aime » about a person, the verb is by itself, so it's pure, it's real, it means a lot.

By adding the « bien », it actually *lowers,* in a sense, the amount of love and makes it similar to a « like ». Je sais, it's maybe a little weird, but does that make any sense now?
— Oui, ça va. C'est magnifique.
— Vraiment?
— Non. But do I have any choice?

Now, we both burst out laughing. It's so good to have ma dear Chloé avec moi.

— Listen Ella, I am saying that because, well, I did notice the way you guys look at each other.
Did she say the way *we* look at each other?
I blush, instantly.

— Ella, it's fine. I know you, tu sais?
— Oui, je sais.
— Do you miss Chad?
Chad. Why did she have to bring him up. Now my eyes are teary, and I can't speak.

— Listen Ella, je sais... et je **comprends**. I understand. You liked Chad, et... we both thought this relationship was going somewhere.

— Oui... we did. I mumble from under my breath.

— We could not have known that his ex-girlfriend would come back into his life. I mean, he was so nice to you.

— Oui, but that was it, he was just nice. Too nice maybe. We should have known. I was his friend.

— Non, Ella, we could not have known. Don't blame yourself.

I am holding back my tears now.

Yes, realizing that Chad was not into me hurt. But I moved on. I even pursued my old and wildest dream of learning le français. Et je suis à Montréal. All on my own. How crazy is that?

— Je suis vraiment désolée about the Chad thing, but, I am proud of you Ella. Je suis **fière** de toi!

Oui, my eyes may still be wet, but at the same time, maybe my heart is glowing and I am breathing, truly breathing, vraiment, for the first time, in a very long time.

I've got this.

27 - VINGT-SEPT :
LES CRÊPES

— Un **café** Ella?

— Oui, merci Monique.

— Une **crêpe**? Monique says, winking at me with that impish smile of hers.

— Une crêpe? Euh… Tempting, I thought, but quickly added: But, j'ai mangé cinq pointes de pizza. C'est… beaucoup! But…

— « But », c'est « **mais** », drops Chloé.

— Merci. C'est beaucoup, « mais »…

— Oui, je sais, c'est beaucoup de pizza, adds Monique cutting in, mais c'est **la fin de semaine**.

— La fin de semaine, c'est le **weekend**… whispers Chloé as she makes a little wall avec sa main, slightly covering her mouth from Monique and says: « It's the same thing. »

— Pour moi, c'est « la fin de semaine », says Monique.

— Pour moi, c'est « le weekend », says Chloé.

Really? Vraiment? Isn't français juste le français

— **Au** Québec, says Monique, on dit « la fin de semaine ».

— **En France**: « le weekend », adds Chloé with a cheeky smile.

— Je comprends. Mais… do I really understand? I guess some ways of speaking can vary between le Québec and la France…

— Oui, c'est différent au Québec et en France.

— Chaque fin de semaine, insists Monique with a chuckle, on mange des **crêpes**, oui? Ella, tu aimes *bien* les crêpes?

I give Chloé a quick glance. « Tu aimes bien »…

Oui, I remember last night's lesson. How could I not.
— Oui, j'aime *bien* les crêpes.

I'm not sure if it was the calory-induced guilt speaking, but I quickly added: « On va faire une randonnée aujourd'hui? » My thinking was, if there is no « grasse matinée » aujourd'hui, no « fat morning », we might as well burn some calories.

I guess my idea of going hiking wasn't very convincing, as both Monique et Chloé didn't seem tempted at all.
— Je fais des crêpes? Monique said quickly without flinching.
— Oui, beaucoup de crêpes! C'est **délicieux**. Et pas de randonnée aujourd'hui. Cholé added.

By now, everyone was just being silly and goofing around. What better way to spend la fin de semaine than having fun, eating some crêpes et laughing with deux other girls. Et, to top it off, tout en français. Je suis fière. Très fière de moi.

Chloé looks at me et says: « Non, aujourd'hui, on ne fait pas de randonnée. Aujourd'hui, on va faire du **patin**! »
— Du patin?
As I wonder what this new word means, I see Monique taking off her slippers, and in her sock feet, she starts sliding on the well polished old hardwood floor, one foot after the other, keeping her back leg up in the air. Her face is serious, as if she was competing in the Olympics, and she ends her charade doing a spin on one foot...
Oh no! Please don't tell me we're going skating aujourd'hui?

« Aujourd'hui, on va faire du patin! »

28 - VINGT-HUIT :
LE PATIN

— Tu es **prête**, Ella?
Am I ready? I will never be ready pour faire du patin. Never.
— Non, je ne suis pas prête.
— Ella, on y va? Insists Chloé.

I grip the bench with both mes mains. I had sat down to put on my rental skates, mes **patins**, but now I don't want to get up.

— Ella, tu viens? Tu viens faire du patin?
— Je... j'arrive dans une minute.

Chloé et Monique are already on the ice, giggling away. Chloé lets out a loud « Ok. On revient dans 2 minutes! » as she grabs la main de Monique and they start skating fast around the rink.

What would I give to be there with them, laughing away, à faire du patin. Instead, je suis ici, alone and scared. I watch them as they disappear into the crowd. I look around me.

This place is amazing. There is a tall Ferris wheel, basically on top of me, I can see the city, and the famous Saint-Laurence River. C'est l'hiver et c'est magnifique. The rink is large, people are skating slowly, some are going fast, but the vibe is chill. Lots of families and groups of friends hanging out. Here I am. Alone. Why do I always put myself in these situations?

*****

« Je... j'arrive dans une minute. »

29 - VINGT-NEUF :
J'AI PEUR

— Ça va?

Who? What? I am just noticing her now. There is an older lady sitting next to me, looking at me intensely. Elle sourit.

— Oui, ça va, merci. I say avec mon best français.

— Tu as froid? She moves a little closer.

— Non, I say with a chuckle, je n'ai pas froid.

— Tu **as peur**?

Oh oh. New word en français. Panic.

The nice lady can see my panic.

— Peur, *it eez* « fear ». She says, articulating each syllable.

Hold on... what? I stay silent as I process this new information. « Tu as froid » is to « have » cold... or to « be » cold, to be exact. So, « tu as peur » is to « have » fear, I guess I should follow the same logic? Does it mean to be afraid? It must be. Now, to answer, I guess I should just switch that for « me ». So instead of the « tu as peur », I should say « **j'ai peur** ». And now, I should change it to the negative form. I feel like I'm proving a complex theorem. And after what seems to be like an eternity, I say, in the slowest possible way: « Non, **je n'ai pas peur** ».

She was staring at me the whole time, holding her breath, as to not disturb my thinking process. The nice lady can finally breathe. Again, elle sourit, as she puts sa main on my arm, she pushes herself up. Standing up, she's about the same size as me sitting down.

— Moi, c'est **Gertrude**. Et toi?
— Moi, c'est Ella.
— C'est bien, Ella. Viens... Tu es prête?

She was one of those people you listen to, no questions asked. There was something about her that made me obey. She had to be an instructor de patin, or a teacher of some kind. Elle était géniale. Elle était in front of me, skating backward, keeping **ses deux mains** in front of me for support. She may have been short, but she was strong and solid.

Et moi? I guess you could say that I was skating. Kind of. I don't think I looked good. But still. I felt amazing.

Et who do I see at that exact moment? Chloé!

— Ella? Génial! Je suis **contente** de te voir faire du patin.
— Chloé, oui, je **fais** du patin. You're glad to see me skating? Moi **aussi**! Me too! In all honesty, I was ecstatic.
Gertrude sourit. Elle dit: « Tu es **douée**, Ella. »

Another panic. I glance at Chloé, silently begging her. In a low voice, she lets out a: « She says you're talented. »
I hear the compliment and blush.
— Oui, Gertrude repeats, tu es très douée.
— Merci Gertrude. Je suis contente de faire du patin avec toi.
— Avec **vous**! Chloé hurriedly adds, you should say « vous ».
— Désolée Gertrude, avec *vous*, I quickly correct my sentence. I wouldn't want to sound disrespectful avec Gertrude.

« Tu es douée, Ella. »

— Le « tu » ça va, kindly replies my newfound teacher.
— Ça va? I ask.
— Oui, ça va.

Oui, **j'ai appris**, I've learned that « vous » should be used with older people, mais Gertrude said le « tu » was fine. I trust her. With her, avec elle, I've learned to skate, j'ai appris à faire du patin. C'est génial.

— C'est *très* génial. I share outloud.
— Désolée Ella, says Chloé with a forced smile. On dit: « C'est *vraiment* génial », et pas « très ».

— Vraiment?
— Oui, really...
— C'est vraiment génial?

Oui, it's more like a question. Le français est **compliqué**. Complicated. So, I look at Chloé et Gertrude et je **dis**: « Le français est vraiment compliqué! »
Elles sourient, both, with a big compassionate smile.

— Oui, **tu as raison**, Ella, says Gertrude, while kindly putting sa main on my shoulder.

I have reason? Son of a biscuit! Help me please, someone! This français is getting more and more compliqué by the second.

Chloé is biting her cheek. I think she finds this funny.

— Ella, remember les **expressions françaises**: « tu as froid, chaud, peur, faim »?

— Oui… j'ai appris ça… avant.

— « Tu as raison » is similar. But, to « have reason », it sorts of means to show reason or logic, to have a point… basically it means that you *are right*.

Gertrude seems lost with all the English spoken. Moi aussi. Me too. And I speak English. Or do I? My brain is turning to mush. I'm getting tired, and now that I am not moving, j'ai froid.

— Merci Chloé, mais on va à la maison? J'ai froid.

— Oui, Ella, tu as raison… Et moi aussi, j'ai froid.

— **Au revoir** Ella. Says Gertrude as she gently grabs my shoulders and gives me a kiss on each cheek. Well, not so much a kiss, as a cheek to cheek embellished with a kissing sound. She's cute. I like her. J'aime bien Gertude.

— Au revoir, Gertrude. I know that « au revoir » is « see you later » and I do not know if I will see her again, but it just seems like the right thing to do. She is just so sweet. So as je souris, I say: « Merci Gertrude de faire du patin avec moi. »

— **De rien.** Tu es très douée.

— Merci. Merci, vraiment! Je sais faire du patin. At this point, I am so excited that I turn back to give her a big hug. She seems surprised, but she hugs me back. Elle sourit.

— Au revoir Ella!

30 - TRENTE :
LE CHOCOLAT CHAUD

Gertrude is now gone. I just want to take off mes patins so Chloé gives me sa main for stability, as we *slooowly* make our way back. Once inside, we go back to our locker. Monique is sitting next to it, daydreaming it seems. She sees us et gets up.
— Ella! Ça va? As she hands each of us each a tissue. She is such a mom, I love that about her.
— Oui, oui! Ça va. Ça va très bien. Merci. Je suis fière.

My legs are shaking. I sit, or more exactly, I crash on the bench. What a day! J'ai froid et j'ai chaud at the same time. Such a weird feeling. Lots of emotions, that's for sure. Honestly, even though avant I didn't want to come, I am happy I came. What an experience. J'ai appris à faire du patin.

— Ella, c'était bien le patin? **Tu as aimé ça**? Asks Chloé.
— Oui, **j'ai aimé** ça. Je suis contente.

Oui, mais, did I like it? Of course I did. Thanks to Gertrude. What a nice woman. People from Québec are the best.
— Oui Chloé, tu as raison, le patin, c'est génial.
— Moi aussi je suis contente, Ella. Mais, tu sais **quoi**?
— What? I mean: quoi?
— J'ai faim. Et **j'ai soif**.
— Quoi? Tu as faim ou **tu as soif**? Are you hungry or thirsty?
— Les deux. **J'ai envie** d'un chocolat chaud.
— You envy quoi?

— Non, « j'ai envie » c'est… Je suis désolée Ella. C'est vraiment compliqué le français! C'est une **expression**…

— Oui, je sais. Comment on dit « j'ai envie » in English?

— It's to have the need, the desire, the craving, not so much the envy, haha! It basically means that I want something.

— **Tu as envie** d'un chocolat chaud? You want some hot chocolate? Me too! Moi aussi!

Et, just like that, a *big* decision is made: on prend un **gros** chocolat chaud et maybe une **collation**? Oui, I admit, my voice might have been an octave higher when I said « moi aussi », as I may have a thing for le chocolat.

Monique brought us to Le Café <u>Olimpico</u>, un café **italien**, not far from where we were. This is definitely the place to be, with a nice mix of people du Québec, et des **touristes**.

— Ella, tu as envie de **commander**?

That's ordering. It has to be. Whoa. My throat feels tight. I'm nervous, mais j'ai envie de commander. Let's do this. On y va.

— **Bonjour. Trois** gros **chocolats chauds, s'il vous plait.** Et aussi, trois biscotti, I quickly add. Good thinking, right? We're not eating de la pizza this time, mais on a faim.

— C'est tout?

— Oui, merci.

— De rien.

I breathe a sigh of relief. It was all so quick. Now I can relax and drink mon chocolat chaud. C'est délicieux. Life is delicious.

« Trois gros chocolats chauds, s'il vous plait. »

31 - TRENTE ET UN :
LE BONHOMME DE NEIGE

Finally. We're home. On est à la maison. What a day! C'était génial aujourd'hui. From le café, we went to la station Place d'Armes, and caught le métro to get home. J'aime bien le métro à Montréal. A quick dix minutes dans le métro et another dix minutes walking dans la neige, et we were à la maison. I was cold, j'avais froid, so I walked fast and ahead of the deux girls. They were chatting away en français aussi, et... j'étais contente d'arriver à la maison. I was happy to get home.

Mais... What is that? C'est quoi? Juste in front of my house, or should I say, la maison de Monique, there is a path, un sentier leading to... a snowman. Holy guacamole! That snowman is huge! Who did that? As I step closer, I notice that his long nose is made of a grosse carrot, his eyes and mouth are made with pebbles, and some small twigs placed above his eyes juste look like long eyelashes. Génial. He is so handsome, standing tall, dans la neige, l'hiver. J'aime bien this gros snowman.

— Tu aimes mon bonhomme? Out of nowhere it seems, I hear Marc's voice. Il était juste behind the snowman. How did I not see him? He's there, all by himself.
— Ton bonhomme? I ask.
— Oui, mon bonhomme de neige. C'est pour toi!

Pour moi? I blush immediately.

« *Tu aimes mon bonhomme de neige?* »

32 – TRENTE-DEUX :
AU REVOIR CHLOÉ

Pas de grasse matinée aujourd'hui. La fin de semaine is over. Aujourd'hui, it's back to school pour moi. Chloé has a work meeting et elle will be staying in a hotel until **son départ**, her departure. I'm not even sure I will see her again.
— Mais oui ma **puce, je vais** te voir avant mon départ, I promise.

J'aime bien when she calls me « ma puce », although it makes no sense, as it would translate to « my flea », but it is used as a cute nickname. Je sais, it sounds weird in English, mais everything sounds better en français.
— I have to work, ma puce… I won't have much time.
— Oui, je comprends. Mais, je vais te voir avant ton départ.

We gave each other the biggest hug ever avant son départ. Even Monique hugged her like an old friend. In fact, they are old friends now. Oh, the warmth of les **Québécois**…

We heard a brief horn from her colleague's car coming to pick her up, warning her to hurry as he was blocking traffic. The neighborhood streets are very narrow and full of parked cars. Typical Montréal.
— Au revoir Chloé! Monique et moi say in unison.

Monique gently puts sa main on my shoulder. Elle sourit. Mais, in her smile, I see so much compassion and kindness.

— Merci Monique, I say.
— Mais, pourquoi?
— Pour tout. For everything.

This woman just doesn't have any idea how much I appreciate her, how much of an impact she has in my life. And, just like that, I leap toward her and we hugged each other too. No, I am not crying… must be a speck in my eye…

✳✳✳✳✳

« Merci pour tout Monique. »

33 – TRENTE-TROIS :
LA CLASSE

I'm back in school. And the first person I see in the hall, is my dear friend from the Netherlands, __Floor__, des __Pays-Bas__.
— Ça va Floor?
— Oui, ça va, merci. Et toi?
— Génial… I declare.

Floor gives me a sideways glance et me sourit.
— Vraiment? Et, who did you see? Floor dit with a chuckle. A certain cutesy boy with deep blue eyes maybe? She adds with a mischievous smile.

— En français, s'il vous plait.
It's __Johanne__. La **professeure** de français. Oh non! We're in trouble. We're supposed to speak français in school. Mais, Johanne sourit. She's reminding us of the rules, with a smile, always.
— Désolée. I quickly respond.
— On va dans la **classe**?
— Oui, on arrive.
We go sit down dans la classe. Everyone's here. Floor, __Angelika__ d'__Allemagne__, __Maria__ du __Mexique__ et, sitting next to her, __Kenji__, du __Japon__. Et, of course, moi, des __États-Unis__.

— Bonjour! Ça va? Asks la professeure Johanne to our group.
— Oui, oui, merci, we answer together.
— Ella, comment était **ta** fin de semaine?

« En français, s'il vous plait. »

Hum... oui, au Québec, on dit « la fin de semaine », et pas « le weekend ». Mais... What will I say? I always get so nervous in front of la classe. C'est normal, I guess.

— Euh... Ma fin de semaine était géniale. Chloé était à Montréal, et on a fait de la raquette et du patin.
— **Ouah**! Tout ça en une fin de semaine? Exclaims Johanne.
— Oui! On a aussi mangé des crêpes et de la pizza. J'ai mangé cinq pointes de pizza. J'avais faim... I admit timidly, et la pizza était délicieuse.
— Ouah! Ella, tu as raison, ta fin de semaine était géniale. Il **faisait** froid?
— Oui, il « **avait** » froid...

I hear some awkward little laughs. Quoi? What did I say? True, « Il faisait » froid is not the same as « il avait » froid. But I don't know comment on dit ça, I'm so confused. Ma professeure Johanne, well aware of my misunderstanding, explains:
« Aujourd'hui, il *fait* froid. En fin de semaine, il *faisait* froid. »

Ah, I get it! « Il faisait » is describing la température in the past tense! I know what to say. I weigh my words carefully and I proudly say: « Oui, il faisait froid. Il faisait moins dix degrés Celsius. Mais moi, je n'avais pas froid. »
— Génial. Vraiment, tu n'avais pas froid, Ella?
— Non, je suis une **vraie** <u>**Québécoise**</u>! Truly a real one, I thought.

Everyone laughed, mais avec moi this time.

34 – TRENTE-QUATRE :
FLOOR

Je suis avec Floor, juste elle et moi, after la classe de français.

— So, Floor, how was your weekend, ta fin de semaine?
— J'ai fait la grasse matinée, she says, giggling as always.
— Lucky you. It's the best. I tried to faire la grasse matinée on Saturday, but I got une grosse surprise. Chloé était ici!
— That is so cool. Je suis très contente pour toi. Hey, talking about une surprise, you heard the news?
— Non… quoi?
— Maria est avec Kenji.
— Avec, avec? Like, they're an item?
— Oui, c'est ça. That's it. Well, I guess so.
— Good. Good for them. They're both great people, they should be great together.

Vraiment, I mean it. Kenji is cute, mais that's it, c'est tout. And to be honest, I'm quite happy alone… working on mon français.

— Floor, comment on dit: I saw?
— Hum… I think it's: « j'ai vu ».
— Yeah, it rings a bell. J'ai vu. Merci.
— De rien. What did you see?
— J'ai vu un bonhomme de neige.
— Tu as fait un bonhomme de neige?
— Non. Marc a fait un bonhomme de neige. Et il a dit: C'est pour toi.

— Oh! Il a dit ça? That's so nice. Marc likes you. Il t'aime bien. He's a good friend, right?

— Oui… C'est ça.

— Ça va Ella? Inquires Floor, tilting her head.

— Mais oui, ça va. I say cheerfully. On va **manger**?

— Manger quoi?

— J'ai envie de pizza. J'ai vraiment faim.

— Moi aussi j'ai faim! On y va?

And, just like that, yet another grosse decision was made. I love eating, what can I say. Et à Montréal, the food is magnifique.

Floor had heard of le **restaurant** italien called **Il Focolaio** which was quite popular, and apparently they made une pizza délicieuse. Since it was juste à une station de métro, we decided we would walk, using the tunnels and stairways in the Underground City à Montréal, pour arriver close to le restaurant.

Why walk inside? Because of la température. Il fait froid. En hiver, il fait très froid à Montréal. Mais, dans this labyrinth of hidden passages under the city, il ne fait pas froid, et on est bien. J'ai appris that there is a whole network of tunnels connecting shopping malls, les **stations** de métro, offices, etc., in total, 33 kilometres of tunnels. That's… beaucoup de miles? I should learn my conversions…

On est arrivées au restaurant en moins de dix minutes. C'était a little compliqué, mais we made it. Ouah! Le restaurant était vraiment busy. Et chaque pizza looked so yummy. Oui, c'était délicieux. J'ai mangé une grosse pizza, all by myself.

Now, je suis à la maison, alone, mais je suis contente; je suis bien. I may briefly see Chloé before she leaves, so I think I should write her a letter, une lettre en français, so I can give it to her avant son départ. This girl is everything to me, elle est tout pour moi.

*****

« Tu as fait un bonhomme de neige? »

35 – TRENTE-CINQ :
LA LETTRE

Bonjour Chloé,

Ça va?

Une semaine à Montréal. Ouah! C'était une grosse surprise. Toi et moi, les deux touristes de Seattle, ici à Montréal. Tu sais, c'était vraiment génial de te voir.

J'ai bien aimé ma fin de semaine avec toi. Comment on dit ça en français de France? ;-) Le weekend? Oui, c'est ça. J'ai aimé « mon weekend ». On a fait de la raquette et du patin, et on a mangé... de tout!

Tu sais, je n'avais pas envie de faire de la raquette, j'avais juste envie de faire la grasse matinée. Mais tu avais raison, j'ai aimé ça, la raquette. C'était bien.

À Cap-Saint-Jacques, c'était magnifique; faire une longue randonnée dans le sentier et voir la neige blanche, c'était vraiment génial. L'hiver est magique au Québec. Oui, il faisait froid; il faisait moins dix degrés, mais je n'avais pas froid. J'avais chaud. On a fait en tout cinq kilomètres de randonnée. Ouah!

On a aussi fait du patin. J'avais peur, mais j'ai appris comment faire avec Gertrude. Et j'étais douée... Gertrude a dit ça, non?

Et on a bien mangé à la maison. Les collations en randonnée, une grosse pizza (elle était délicieuse), et Monique a fait des crêpes. Elle est vraiment géniale. J'aime beaucoup Monique.

Au café italien, toi, tu avais faim et soif, et moi, j'ai appris à commander des chocolats chauds et des biscottis pour nous trois. Tout en français. J'étais fière de moi.

J'ai aussi vu un gros bonhomme de neige, il était magnifique, et il était, euh, juste pour moi, a dit Marc. Ah... Marc et son chocolat délicieux.

En fin de semaine, j'ai appris beaucoup d'expressions françaises avec toi. Ensuite, en classe, j'ai vu ma professeure Johanne, et aussi Floor, Angelika, Maria et Kenji. J'aime bien ma classe. Je ne comprends pas tout le français, mais ça va.

Chloé, merci pour la surprise. Vraiment, merci beaucoup. J'étais contente de te voir. Avant, c'était compliqué pour moi, mes deux longues semaines à Montréal, avec le français et tout. Tu sais, j'avais vraiment envie de te voir. Avec toi, tout va bien. Avant, j'étais une touriste, et aujourd'hui, je suis vraiment bien ici. J'aime Montréal. Je suis une vraie Québécoise. :-)

Au revoir.

Ta puce,

Ella

« *Bonjour Chloé. Ça va?* »

LA FIN

(THE END)

GLOSSARY

WORDS, EXPRESSIONS	MEANING	PAGE
1. Montréal	Montreal (proper noun)	9
2. avant	before	10
3. Seattle	Seattle (proper noun)	
4. français	French (m)	
5. à	at, to, in, until	
6. il	he, it (m)	
7. elle	she, it (f)	
8. Ella	Ella (proper noun)	
9. oui	yes	
10. ça va? ça va	you ok? how are you? fine, good	
11. Monique	Monique (proper noun)	
12. viens	Come; imperative/present, with JE, TU	11
13. faire	to do, to make	
14. la	the (f)	
15. grasse	fat (f)	
16. matinée	morning (f)	
17. faire la grasse matinée	to sleep in, to sleep late	
18. j'	"I" (in front of vowel & muted "h")	
19. arrive	arrive, reach; used with JE, IL, ELLE, ON	
20. des	contraction DE+LES; of the, from, some (pl)	12
21. raquettes	snowshoes (fpl)	

22. tu	you (informal)	
23. non	no	
24. je	I (first person, singular)	
25. les	the (pl)	
26. une	a, an, one (f)	
27. main	hand (f)	
28. ma	my (f)	
29. j'ai	I have	
30. surprise	surprise (f), surprised (f)	
31. tu as	you have	
32. grosse	big, large (f)	
33. Chloé	Chloé (proper noun)	14
34. française	French (f)	
35. sourit	smiles; used with IL, ELLE, ON	
36. te	you, to you, yourself (informal)	
37. voir	to see	
38. je viens te voir	I come to see you, I'm coming to see you	
39. accent	accent (m)	
40. en	in, to, of, some	
41. bien	well, fine, good	
42. tout	all, everything	
43. tout va bien	everything is fine, all is well	
44. suis	am, used with JE	
45. vacances	vacation, holidays (f)	
46. mon	my (m)	
47. semaine	week (f)	
48. génial	great (m)	15

49. pour	for, to	
50. deux	two, 2	
51. semaines	week (fpl)	
52. juste	just, only	
53. longue	long (f)	
54. de	of, from, by	
55. est	is, used with IL, ELLE, ON, CELA (C')	
56. géniale	great (f)	
57. vient	comes; used with IL, ELLE, ON	
58. très	very	
59. et	and	17
60. moi	me, personally, as for me, myself	
61. toi	you, as for you, yourself	
62. raquette	snowshoe, snowshoeing (f)	
63. vraiment	really, truly, definitely, for sure	
64. on	somebody, someone, we (informal)	18
65. va	goes, is going; used with IL, ELLE, ON	
66. on va	we are going to	
67. faire de la raquette	to go snowshoeing	
68. on va faire de la raquette	we're going snowshoeing	
69. l'	the (LA, LE) in front of a voyel & muted h	
70. hiver	winter (m)	
71. souris	smile; imperative/present, used with JE, TU	
72. Communauto	Communauto (proper noun)	20
73. Marc	Marc (proper noun)	
74. hum	hmm!	
75. chéri	cute nickname: darling, sugar, honey (m)	

76. fait	does, makes; used with IL, ELLE, ON	
77. chaque	each, every	
78. aujourd'hui	today	21
79. avec	with	
80. nous	we (formal)	
81. Cap-Saint-Jacques	Cap-Saint-Jacques (proper noun)	
82. j'ai invité	I have invited, I invited	
83. c'est	it is, that is, this is, it's	
84. dans	in, inside, into	
85. minutes	minutes (pl)	
86. ici	here	
87. neige	snow	22
88. magique	magical (m) (f)	
89. blanche	white (f)	
90. on est arrivées	we have arrived, we arrived (fpl)	23
91. heure	hour, o'clock (f)	
92. collations	snacks (fpl)	
93. ensuite	then, afterwards, after	
94. prends	take; imperative/present, used with JE, TU	
95. photo	photo (f)	
96. prend	takes; used with IL, ELLE, ON	
97. nos	our (pl)	
98. les	before a verb: them	24
99. revient	comes back; used with IL, ELLE, ON	
100. tu es	you are; used with TU	
101. cinq	cinq, 5	26
102. kilomètres	kilometres, kilometers (mpl)	

103. randonnée	hike, walk, trek (f)	
104. j'ai fait	I have done, I did, I have made, I made	
105. d'abord	first, firstly	
106. chérie	darling, sugar, honey (f)	
107. froid	cold (m)	
108. j'ai froid	(lit: "I have cold") I am cold	
109. photos	photos (pl)	
110. un	a, an, one, 1 (m)	
111. couteau	knife (m)	
112. suisse	Swiss, of Switzerland	
113. couteau suisse	Swiss army knife (m)	
114. touriste	tourist (m/f)	27
115. normal	normal, usual habitual (m)	
116. Québec	Quebec (proper noun)	
117. on y va	let's go, we're off, here we go	
118. le	the (m)	
119. sentier	path, way (m)	
120. grosses	big, large (fpl)	28
121. tu as froid	(lit: "you have cold") you are cold	
122. brrr	brr !	
123. il fait froid	it is cold, freezing	
124. ne... pas	not, don't, doesn't	
125. je n'ai pas froid	I am not cold, I don't feel cold	
126. minute	minute (f)	
127. magnifique	magnificent (m) (f)	
128. heures	hours, o'clock (pl)	29
129. température	temperature (f)	

130. moins	less, fewer, minus	
131. dix	ten, 10	
132. degrés	degrees (mpl)	
133. moins dix degrés	minus ten degrees	
134. Celsius	Celsius	
135. manges	Eat; present, used with TU	31
136. tu ne manges pas	you don't eat, you're not eating	
137. euh	uh!	
138. j'ai mangé	I have eaten, I ate	
139. mes	my (pl)	
140. du	contraction of DE+LE; of the, some (m)	
141. chocolat	chocolate (m)	
142. merci	thank you, thanks (m)	
143. chaud	hot, warm (m)	32
144. chaude	hot, warm (f)	
145. j'ai chaud	(lit: "I have hot") I'm hot, I feel hot	
146. différent	different (m)	36
147. était	was; used with IL, ELLE, ON, CELA (C')	
148. c'était	it was, that was, this was	
149. ce n'était pas	it was not, that was not, this was not	
150. sa	his, her (f)	37
151. faim	hunger (f)	
152. j'ai faim	(lit: "I have hunger") I am hungry	
153. tu as faim	(lit: "you have hunger") you are hungry	
154. beaucoup	a lot	39
155. pizza	pizza (f)	
156. délicieuse	delicious (f)	

157. comment	how, how to, in what way	
158. on	informal we, someone, or general 'you'	
159. dit	says; used with IL, ELLE, ON	
160. comment on dit	how to say, how do you/we say	
161. pointes	point, slice (of pizza, round cake) (fpl)	
162. désolée	sorry (f)	41
163. tu aimes	you love, you like; used with TU	
164. j'aime	I love, like; also used with JE, IL, ELLE, ON	
165. sais	I/you know (how), I'm/you're aware	
166. comprends	understand; used with JE, TU	43
167. fière	proud (f)	
168. café	coffee (m)	44
169. crêpe	crepe, thin pancake (f)	
170. mais	but	
171. fin	end (f)	
172. semaine	week (f)	
173. fin de semaine	weekend (m)	
174. weekend	weekend -anglicism (m)	
175. au	contraction of À+LE; at the, to the, with	
176. en	in, to, of, some	
177. France	France (f)	
178. crêpes	crepe, thin pancake (pl)	
179. délicieux	delicieux (m) (mpl)	45
180. patin	skate, skating (m)	
181. prête	ready (f)	47
182. patins	skates (m)	
183. peur	fear (f)	49

184. tu as peur	(lit: "you have fear") you are afraid	
185. j'ai peur	I am afraid	
186. je n'ai pas peur	I am not afraid	
187. Gertrude	Gertrude (proper noun)	50
188. ses	his, her (pl)	
189. contente	happy, pleased, glad (f)	
190. fais	do, make; imperative/present, with JE, TU	
191. aussi	too, also, as well	
192. douée	gifted, talented (f)	
193. vous	you (formal or plurial)	
194. j'ai appris	I have learned, I learned	52
195. compliqué	complicated (m)	
196. dis	say; imperative/present, with JE, TU	
197. elles	they (f)	
198. sourient	smile; present, with ILS, ELLES	
199. raison	reason (f)	
200. tu as raison	(lit: "you have reason") you are right	
201. expressions	expressions (fpl)	53
202. françaises	French (fpl)	
203. au revoir	goodbye, bye for now	
204. rien	nothing	
205. de rien	you're welcome, don't mention it	
206. tu as aimé	you liked, you enjoyed	54
207. ça	that, this, it	
208. j'ai aimé	I liked, I loved, I enjoyed	
209. quoi	what	
210. soif	thirst (f)	

211. j'ai soif	(lit: "I have thirst") I am thirsty	
212. tu as soif	you are thirsty	
213. envie	longing, desire (f)	
214. j'ai envie	I want to, I feel like	
215. expression	expression (f)	55
216. tu as envie	you want to, you feel like	
217. gros	big, large (m) (mpl)	
218. collation	snack (f)	
219. Olimpico	Olimpico (proper noun)	
220. italien	Italien (m)	
221. touristes	tourists (mpl) (fpl)	
222. commander	to order	
223. bonjour	good morning, good afternoon, good day	
224. trois	three, 3	
225. chocolats	chocolats (mpl)	
226. chauds	hot (mpl)	
227. s'il	if it/he	
228. vous	you (formal)	
229. plait	pleases	
230. s'il vous plait	(lit: "if it pleases you") please (formal)	
231. maison	house (f)	57
232. à	at, to, in, untill	
233. à la maison	at home, in the house	
234. station	station, stop (f)	
235. Place d'Armes	Place d'Armes (proper noun)	
236. métro	metro, subway, tube (m)	
237. avais	had; used with JE, TU	

238. étais	was, were: used with JE, TU	
239. d'	of, from (DE) in front of a voyel or muted h	
240. arriver	to arrive, to get to, to reach	
241. bonhomme	man, guy (m)	
242. ton	your (m)	
243. bonhomme de neige	snowman (m)	
244. son	his, her (m)	59
245. départ	departure (m)	
246. puce	flea (f)	
247. ma puce	my sweety, my darling	
248. je vais	I am going to	
249. Québécois	Quebecer, Quebecker (proper noun) (m)	
250. Floor	Floor (proper noun)	61
251. Pays-Bas	Netherlands (proper noun)	
252. Johanne	Johanne (proper noun)	
253. professeure	teacher (f)	
254. classe	class, lesson (f)	
255. Angelika	Angelika (proper noun)	
256. Allemagne	Germany (proper noun)	
257. Maria	Maria (proper noun)	
258. Mexique	Mexico (proper noun)	
259. Kenji	Kenji (proper noun)	
260. Japon	Japan (proper noun)	
261. États-Unis	United States (proper noun)	
262. ta	your (f)	
263. ouah	wow!	63
264. faisait	did, made; used with IL, ELLE, ON	

265. avait	had; used with IL, ELLE, ON	
266. vraie	true, real, genuine (f)	
267. Québécoise	Quebecer, Quebecker (proper noun) (f)	
268. j'ai vu	I have seen, I saw	64
269. il a dit	he has said, he said	
270. manger	to eat	65
271. restaurant	restaurant (m)	
272. Il Focolaio	Il Focolaio (proper noun)	
273. stations	stations, stops (fpl)	

The letter

Hello Chloé,

How are you?

A week in Montreal. Wow, that was a big surprise. You and me, the two tourists from Seattle, here in Montreal. You know, it was really great to see you.

I really enjoyed my weekend with you. How do you say that in French? ;-) The weekend? Yes, that's it. I loved "my weekend". We went snowshoeing and skating, and ate... everything!

You know, I didn't feel like snowshoeing, I just felt like sleeping in. But you were right, I liked it, snowshoeing. It was great.

At Cap-Saint-Jacques, it was magnificent; a long hike on the trail, and seeing the white snow... It was really great. Winter is magical in Quebec. Yes, it was cold; it was minus ten degrees (Celsius), but I wasn't cold. I was warm. We hiked a total of five kilometres. Wow!

We also went skating. I was scared, but I learned how to do it with Gertrude. And I was good... Gertrude said that, didn't she?

And we ate well at home: hiking snacks, a big pizza (it was delicious), and Monique made pancakes. She's really great. I really like Monique.

At the Italian café, you were hungry and thirsty, and I learned how to order hot chocolates and biscotti for the three of us. All in French. I was so proud of myself.

I also saw a big snowman, it was beautiful, and it was, uh, just for me, said Marc. Ah... Marc and his delicious chocolate.

At the end of the week, I learned a lot of French expressions with you. Then, in class, I saw my teacher Johanne, and also Floor, Angelika, Maria and Kenji. I like my class. I don't understand all the French, but that's okay.

Chloé, thank you for the surprise. Really, thank you so much. I was so happy to see you. It used to be complicated for me, my two long weeks in Montreal, with the French and everything. You know, I really wanted to see you. With you, everything's fine. I used to be a tourist, and now I really like it here. I love Montreal. I'm a true Quebecer :-)

Goodbye.

Your "flea" (your sweety)

Ella

Made in the USA
Coppell, TX
04 July 2025

51472828R00049